Doppelgänger

Poems & Prose

Reading Instructions:

To be read with a safety pin heart

Doppelgänger

Poems & Prose

K.M. Littleworth

Published 2023 Safety Pin Heart

ISBN: 978-1-3999-4319-2

All poetry & prose by K.M. Littleworth
Copyright © K.M. Littleworth 2023

Cover photography by Lara Howe Photography
Copyright © Lara Howe Photography 2023

K.M. Littleworth asserts the moral right to be identified as the author of this work.

All rights reserved.

Witness Me!! Character names respectfully referenced from Mad Max Fury Road 2015 and Mad Max 2 1981

No part of this book or cover may be reproduced or used in any manner without the prior permission from the publisher except for quotation in a book review, discussion or for educational purposes.

Official Author Website: www.kmlittleworth.com

For Lara & Kit

Contents

Doppelgänger   13
Surf Shack Chique   14
Schtum   15
Spatula Bachelor   16
Bin   18
Higgledy-Piggledy   19
The Borough Council Louts   20
Forgazi   21
Rustic   22
Stickle Brick Meet and Greet   23
We've Not Come Far   24
I Shout Louder   25
Mediabook   26
Jeeves and Wanker   27
High Staines Drifter   28
Just A Half Sermon   29
Revised Fare   30
Olly's Allegro   32
Badass Bluetit   33
After Party   34
Clock Watcher   36
Brains!   38
Big Baby   39

Tarantula   41
Etrosion 21   42
Soulless   43
Uncomfortable   44
Shrapnel   45
Jolly Green Giants   46
Kensington Avenue   47
Dolly   48
As Is   49
Bungee   50
Nihilism by Mouth   51
Massacre   52
Synchronicity   53
The 4:15 Kick   54
There Shall Be No Place   56
Bones and Tar   57
X   58
Mr Preegles   61
94!   62
Cardiac College   63
Two Footed Challenge   64
Fashionista   66
When in Roam   67
Bricks and Mortar   68
Pine   70
Pudding Pocket   71
Twickenham   72
Spider On a Recce   74
Hokey Dina!   77

Pro Rata Tomatoes   78
Dawkin Kettleton's Spuds   79
BOLT   80
Photostagenic   81
Ready for the Ride   82
Oval   83
Loud Silence   84
A Breezy Poem   85
Medusa   86
Intruder   87
Morse Code   88
The Warmth of Galahad   89
Loungeroom Love   90
Red Curtain Call   93
Her   94
Lemon Drizzle Cake   95
Commune   96
Cooper   97
Hellova Novella   98
Love is a Rabid Dog   101
Witness Me!!   102
Farm   104
Climbing Frame Fall   105
Frankie the Fixer   106
Safety Pin Heart   109

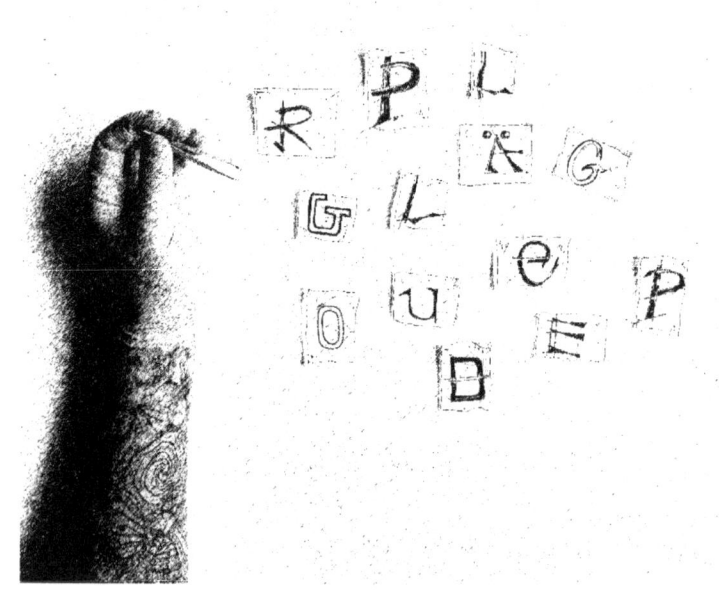

Doppelgänger

An apparition or a person's living double,
Summed up by a single German word,
"I could have sworn I saw you yesterday!"
Is something that I've often heard.

There must be a carbon copy about,
My so-called whereabouts is always wrong,
I was sat at home keeping myself to myself,
And I've been here all along.

"But I bellowed your name from across the street,
I'm sure you did glance then turn your head!"
Once again, a case of mistaken identity,
I was flued-up, chicken-souping in bed.

"Well how about Monday on the night bus,
Same jacket, same beard, same hair?"
I was curled up on the sofa scribbling this poem,
Out late on a weekday? I wouldn't dare!

And just to warn you in advance for the weekend,
The drunken rascal on the town won't be me,
Singing and staggering out of bookies and bars,
My Doppelgänger is who you did just see.

Surf Shack Chique

Up it come from a shack down on the south coast,
For an extra two quid it was in next day's post,
I looked a right proper dapper dandy I must boast,
To my neon surf shack chique I raise a toast.

A family member said the material was ever so nice,
It was in the winter sale at a fair old price,
Now I gotta' grow dude hair and avoid head lice,
Go get a little neon surf shack chique is my advice.

I'd be point-breaking this weekend if only I could,
But the beach is sixty miles from my neighbourhood,
You can catch me in the canal riding a piece of wood,
Surf shack chique neon is now the colour of my blood.

Schtum

Are they an ignoramus or an ignorant anus?
I can't quite decide,
Stunt-cutting me mid-sentence,
Jackal-nipping at my stride.

And when they've ceased rattling,
Flighty attentions turned back my way,
I'll stand in dignified silence,
They don't deserve to hear what I have to say.

Perhaps they'll conclude, that I'm being mighty rude,
Maybe awkward, defiantly smug,
But they chose to smother, a mild mannered brother,
Who'll no longer be taken for a mug!

Spatula Bachelor

Once the DVD, vinyl and CD collection,
Were sat at their alphabetical best,
I decided to say Hi, to the white goods supplied,
For my first major culinary test.

With budget saucer, plate and bowl,
The good Mr Kipling supplied a tart,
I was to have a bash, at a spicey corned beef hash,
Gulping nervously, on the microwave I pushed start.

Piping hot n'easy comfort grub,
Nuked, slopped and devoured without hitch,
But I knew this would never do, when dining for two,
These five minute pingers I would have to ditch.

A hustling bustling City centre shopping spree,
God help that credit card bill,
I was like a pack horse, bags of pans, food and sauce,
Eager to simmer, fry, boil, bake and grill.

I temporarily swapped my beloved sports channel,
For shows with chefs and tantalisingly tasty ideas,
No need to swerve, any dish I wish to serve,
In the rear view mirror were my old cooking fears.

Poached eggs with white fluffy steaming surround,
Dropped onto a perfect pineappled gammon hock,
No longer a joke, when you forked open that runny yolk,
A saliva inducing treat no critic could ever mock.

Soy, sizzle and Sake that stir-fry,
Salt, lemon and butter that plaice,
Dice peppers with a knife, stir risotto for your life,
All with a newfound smile on your face.

The key ingredient though, in every successful dish,
Is to season liberally whilst on heat,
Chilli and turmeric, mixed herbs and cinnamon sticks,
And always remember to rub your meat!

Bin

A big burley burning bin,
All amber orange and rusty tin,
I make lots of paper and plastic friends,
But as quick as we meet they leave again.
I told them to hide behind the cornflake box,
Last night's paper and a bag of old socks,
Had no sooner we carried out the plan we did hatch,
Along came a rotter and struck up a match!

Higgledy–Piggledy

All higgledy-piggledy messy and jaunty,
Disorganized disarranged
dishevelled bedraggled deranged
slap dashed slovenly and naughty,
I do believe it's time for a good sorty.

I'm lethargically lackadaisical inactive and inert,
Boring bone-idly shiftless
languorous leisurely listless
slothful and work-shyly overt,
I better pull up my socks and launder a shirt.

Ever so unkempt unbrushed matted and mucky,
Nit-liced grunged potty grotty
undernourished untamed knotty
mangled tangled mangey and strewn,
Have you been using Vidal-Baboon?

The Borough Council Louts

They're skimming the till and my wages
Hasn't been a copper seen around here for ages
You can find these buggers in the yellow pages
The Borough Council louts.

The binmen always did an absolute sterling job
But the three bin recycling sin was created by a nob
Saving our planet? They were on the bloody rob
The Borough Council louts.

I've got a modest house on a modest street
Trying to find my feet with a sixty-hour week
I tore open my quarterly and let out a shriek!
The Borough Council louts.

I pay the same as folk blessed with a half a mil' home
Because this old mining village is in the wrong zone
Good luck with customer service cretins on the phone
The Borough Council louts.

Hug a hoodie and silence the residents
Meek Police call Neighbourhood Watch a vesicant
Only when it hit the papers, they finally set a precedent
Buying round here? I'd be bloody hesitant!
The ruddy Borough Council louts!

Forgazi

Ever dabbled with a Dalí or meddled with a Miró?
A Raphael ruse to reach the auction hall,
Forest thick raise of hands, my Degarthe in demand,
Mr Mimeo enchants another country manor wall.

I study the great artists and the great art of deceit,
A wizard of the watercolour, a canvass connoisseur,
Exceedingly fine, with every stroke and line,
Collectors ravage a Monet morsal, no cynic could deter.

I dig and dissolve deep dupable prosperous pockets,
Like an ox hair de-colouring in an acetone jar,
Museums parade for years, a Picasso to bring tears,
As trusty tourists travel from afar.

I pigment punk professionals with a plausible pallet,
An art imitator outlaw, that many are sure to deplore,
But a sincere promise to you, this confessional be true,
Or have you read this little poem, somewhere before?

Rustic

Try a pasty from Cambridgeshire Valley's pantry,
Pastry puffed with Holme Fen height love,
Precision placed in a daisy adorned doyley,
Delivered by bicycle by Benjamin the baker's boy…
To Welcome Break services, junction 16.

Fancy fondling a fresh loaf from Farmfield's Farmhouse Farm?
Windmill white fluffy flour, dough knuckle-kneaded,
Slices Courteously hand carved for door stopper tea n' toast decadence,
Cushioned upon a loose grain horse cart, negotiating narrow sun-kissed Cumbrian trail…
Two for a quid at the Co-operative.

Or how about a bulging BBQ banquet by The Blossom Village Butchers?
Neither a fleck of blood or fly to be seen with this well-oiled mechanical meat machine,
All ribs, rosettes, rosy cheeks, wax paper pork and leek smiles, produce that'll keep and travel for miles…
Complimentary aqua with every poultry portion.

Stickle Brick Meet and Greet

There must be a tad more to life than a stickle brick meet and greet? Some here for coffee cake and a skive, I know they'll applaud the claptrap and unfortunately there's nowhere to hide as common sense becomes commodity most showcase synergy and oddity with no heart passion pride or drive.

The fickle fan on the wall is a necessity to waft waffle whilst the water dispenser in the hall moistens dry fibbing throats, you'll have to shake hands with a limp gripped accessor excuse the pickup lines of this pretentious pecker for he knows not what he does, literally.

With treble Windsor wolf woven wellies perched near the projector try not to projectile at the jibber-jabber the buzzword baron, oh lord take me now here comes the JIT system...

Hyperlocal freemium digital transformation
thought leader omnichannel personalization
advertainment value-added gamification
behavioural retargeting KPI disruptive innovation,
He's a bit of a tinker this blue sky thinker.

There's more to life, than a stickle brick meet and greet. Just look at these poor clients, who've voted with their feet.

We've Not Come Far

A real glassed from the past
I require six stitches and a doner kebab
You never see a tét à tét over a simple thé au lait

We've not come far
From that saloon door Stetsoned silhouette
Shot of red eye slid along the bar
Close but no cigar, designer stubble and cigarette

Stumble with sheer Brute Sherman sex appeal
No socked loafers chewing gum and chunder heels
Illegible nightclub stamp on hand in high demand

We've not come far
From bow-tied supplied bulldogs on watch
Names not down knots and needles in arse cheeks
Go up a notch, golden handshakes and vintage scotch

There's a giant glitch in the glamour and the glitz
Clucking fried chicken instead of dinner at the Ritz
We've definitely not come far
The nightlife in this shitty City is quite simply the pits

I Shout Louder

I was a quiet young lad and my skates were Bauer,
The milk from my school was unpleasantly sour,
Scribble and scribing in my room hour after hour,
With a pad and pen I shout louder.

I was taught, torn up and graded by nitwit doubters,
Their hard-on for art was a vase of fucking flowers,
When I sketched for myself I had superpowers,
With a pad and pen I shout louder.

I created a greater din than Leslie Crowther,
Selling my first painting I couldn't have been prouder,
I'd drown out a Ferrari driven by the great Niki Lauder,
With a pad and pen I shout louder.

I said…
With a pad and pen I shout louder,

One more time…
With a pad and pen and a large glass of Black Tower…
I Shout **LOUDER!!**

Mediabook

Walk right by, why don't you
Barely a fleeting look
I thought we were bosom buddies?!
with a million other muckers on Mediabook

I don't ask for much
perhaps even a smile or just a nod
Looks like you live a life online
Friend collecting Media sod.

'Oh' here we all are!' yells a family pic post
'My goodness haven't they grown!'
'Many thanks' types an unscrupulous stranger
Peeping at your family and blueprint of home

'CHEERS! Everybody back in England!'
'Looks lovely, make sure you have one for me!'
'I certainly will' breathes another well-wisher
Climbing out of your window with jewellery and tv!

Jeeves and Wanker

Tea and titties Mr Belford?
Well I don't mind if I do,
Would you purr at a Whores-D'oeuvre,
Followed by a Caligula stew at two?

Pardon me Sir, the seamstress is here,
To assist with your ever expanding wilt,
Send her right up, the needle fingered buttercup,
I'll show her how Mighty Blighty was built.

A snifter of Brandy and a Montecristo?
The hobnobbery of the charity event in full swing,
Embrace the jazz band, pearl spoon of caviar in hand,
Escort all donations to the private wing, to sing.

I think maybe we're perhaps close to war Sir?
Possibly a good time to address the troops?
Everything's fine, I demand substances and wine,
Then I'll brown envelope our cahoots in Jack Boots.

High Staines Drifter

Water pistol and wet t-shirt,
The ladies are all on high alert,
Just caned six pints and he's become a flirt,
The High Staines Drifter.

With looky looky Rolex and cap on his head,
Should have really bought the straw Stetson instead,
He loves his annual booze up in the Med,
The High Staines Drifter.

Counterfeit Camels, he's a super polluter,
Bumbag instead of a six shooter,
Hi-Ho silver he crashed a hired scooter,
I wish he would just use his computer,
The High Staines Drifter.

Just A Half Sermon

You're getting a little low there chap,
Fancy same again?
The night's merely a youngster,
It's barely half past ten!..

Oh, go on, just a half.

I believe it's my round matey,
What you gonna' be having?
Don't worry about your blood shot eyes,
And the fact that you are slathering…

Oh, go on, just a half.

Definitely my twist big lad,
Last round, swear on my life!
If the old ball n' chain kicks you out for being late,
Just chop her in for a pub friendly wife...

Oh, go on, just a half.

Leaving early Captain? Celebrating here!
It's my birthday, haven't you been told?
Although, I've used this one so many times now,
I must be at least one hundred years old!...

Oh, go on… make it a pint!

Revised Fare

My arm, rigid and signpost straight, blesses with one
hundred yards grace. The moon dances off my Sekonda
and signet ring, as it approaches with haste.
Are Sandra and Keanu aboard?
I'm nervous, yet well-schooled.
The timetable behind cracked and fag end scolded
perspex studied twice.
My bottom does the five pence – fifty pence dance as I'm
fully aware of the potential consequences.
If I miss it, or it misses me... twenty-seven minutes until
the next one. Extremity is called upon.
I lean out a little. A provocative Converse intrudes the
bus lane tarmac. Surely just a matter of time?

And the shelter?... stainless and lit up like a space hub,
And me?... contorting like a demented hitchhiker,
And then?...
The screech of realisation and the scent of burning brake
pad blubber.
I stand before the 'Stand Clear' shields, that hiss and
creak back on unloved hydraulics.
My tummy cramps and twists as I contemplate the real
price of my pickup. It's crude abruptness.
Are there any injuries? Are there students on the upper
deck now baying for blood with cider and black laps?!

Fortunately, I'm embraced by the driver and his fuzzy
warmth, charming me with an aggressive critique of my
winter wardrobe. A mid-thigh length darkish coat in
November is apparently 'Beggars Belief!'

He has a stir about him, jilted almost.
Perhaps a product of the system, long hours, short pay, bullied, broken and banished into the wilderness. The unfamiliarity and unpredictability of the outer village Badlands… 'Where no two pensioner be the same'. They all surf silver, but are altered, engineered with artificial parts, Metals, ceramics and plastics. False hip joints, teeth and the occasional pacemaker.

Perhaps his trophy wife parted ways on announcement of his ring road route loss. Then shacked up with a whippersnapper, a real flyboy of the number forty-eight. City centre wind in tousled hair, petrol station deal wraparound sunglasses, pocket radio playing on the dash and an extra tanned right elbow. A rebel.

Or perhaps he's just a bit of a twat.

Either way, I request the innocent "Single to town, please." And double digit dig for two solitary pound coins. It's no use. Just a shrapnel soup of small silver and copper. I feel the piercing gaze of impatient passengers.
He glares at me with sulphur eyes of recognition.
He's seen me before.
He knows I'm no tourist.
He knows that I should know the drill!
The air suffocates with anticipation as a single bead trickles down from the clutch of perspiration gathering on my brow. Taking in a deep breath I sinfully mumble…
"Can I pay with a fiver?"

Olly's Allegro

Obscene A-Team black and red,
Pristine Springsteen Old Glory roof,
Liquid molasses go fast stripe,
A Max Power mukbang,
SX Quatro TDI XR 1.1 Litre R-Type.

Mod as you will, Nova thrill,
To the next lights, text your last rights,
Quadruple exhausts, 50 mph, no horse G-Force,
Four in the back, baseball cap, watch him go,
But they still got nothing on Olly's Allegro.

It was his dad's, shoddy brake pads,
Presented in onlooker frown, diarrhoea brown,
A big reveal, was the square steering wheel,
Sheer bliss no power assist,
Neither cd, mp3, just an old wireless of 80's honesty,
On the open road, Olly was classically free.

Badass Bluetit

I'm up to my fairy elbows
Degreasing an Everest of pots
Easing my burden is the kitchen sink window
Watching the birdfeeders attacked in flocks

I only replenished this morning
My nuts emptied, and seed is low
They're gonna' bankrupt me these birdies
A visit to the pet shop thirty quid a throw

As the backdoor opens, they scatter the sky
Taking refuge in tree, shrub and bush
I fill the feeders then Hitchcockianally creep away
Under watchful eye of sparrow, blackbird and thrush

I become one with the shadowy patio rear
Eager to see who will brave it first
There's a chatter and a cheap, the din of nearing dinner
From out of the foliage the badass bluetit does burst!

After Party

Knock two times on the ceiling if you want me,
Everyone's sloshed and on the dancefloor,
Uncle Gerald had a fright, it's nearly midnight,
He's got a belly full of ale but he wants more.

My John J Cousin, red tie around his head,
Throwing fizz-induced shapes for one and all,
His daughter Lucy, has been real boozy,
Wedding breakfast sprayed up the toilet wall.

Blend in with the backdrop and inconspicuously sip,
No use my friend, nobody is safe,
"Let's have everybody up!" yells the DJ with a gut,
Where's my plasters, shoes are starting to chafe.

Staggering to the dancefloor, is blue rinse Ethel,
Move over youngsters with legs, lips, lashes and tan,
Cheese-a classics do play, the oldie does sway,
From now on we'll have to call her Insta-gran.

Tik-Tok-Tik, a choreographed prance,
The it couple limelight in matching green dress and tie,
Revellers form a circle, around bridesmaids of purple,
If they Can Can, watch out for a stiletto in the eye!

The energy juiced adrenaline fused photographer,
Craftily chameleons and clicks away,
Our giddy groom, plays football with a stray balloon,
Nephew twice removed, stalks any single female prey!

The overheads flicker on, taxis impatiently wait,
All war-torn Wedonist's complexions are seen,
The ginned up bride does cry- as they never played Summer Of 69,
Afraid there's no more dry ice left in the smoke machine.

A bloodshot, vice temple crushing bonce-Bonjour,
Hazy missing steps, all being Poirotly traced,
Everyone grated and deflated, Gimme' juice I'm dehydrated!,
Le petit dejeuner to be enjoyed with guests rouge faced.

Clock Watcher

It's ten past bloody one
I know where I belong
Dream cruising in a Lambo'
Licence plate NODLAND-1
With a top hat and cane
A sky of laser rain
Off a cliff I swerve, only to be jolted awake once again!

It's just hit two
What am I gonna' do?
This ageing bladder woke me up
Right on cue
With fluffy slipper feet
I'll get up and admit defeat
It's always an achievement at this hour, if I miss the seat!

It's just after three
No sleep for me
I blame the monk- spring mattress
And my late chippy tea
Tossing to the left, then rolling to right,
Duvet putting up quite a fight
There's an inconsiderate wolf moon, howling through the Skylight.!

It's half past four
No sleep ya'll
Just dreamt I was a cowboy with a Texan drawl
My Morgan buckaroo'd on the great terrain
A dusty thud and I was in the land of the living once
Again!

Oh man alive
It's five past five
If I don't drop off soon
I'll be too zonked to drive
As a student I'd indulge
The sleep provider cider
But I was twenty years younger
Three stone lighter
Can't believe I'm forced to pull another all-nighter!

Oh bollocks, it's nearly six!
Time for the alarm to get its sadistic kicks!
I'll be in the shit, if I call in sick
So, I'll just have to hit snooze
And for one hour's clean sleep I'll pray…
Hold on a second!...
Is today Saturday?!!

Brains!

Better hit the street with fleeting feet
But be calm, caffeinated and collected
A government surpass, fill the tank with gas
Fender off all frenzied and infected

It's a closed gate on the Interstate
Burn through backwoods, bayou and beyond
A glovebox of trinkets and cash, radio on the dash
Eager for other survivors to respond

Fancy a munch, there's an apocalypse pack lunch
Roast beef and radish on rye bread
For desert buttered scone, but if bitten later on
We'll all be feasting on brains instead!

Big Baby

It was a proud day for Mr and Mrs Nebula, 4.6 million years ago,

As they stood beaming in the maternity ward at their new arrival in the Galaxy incubator below.

The good midwife, Nurse Big Bang took a shine and proclaimed he was a welcome addition to fill a void,

Amongst her other deliveries that day were Solar System, Star, Planet, Moon and Asteroid.

All that was needed now was a name, for this hydrogen cherub of two octillion tonne,

They only knew if it were to be a girl, she would be named Jupiter, so they simply decided to call their son… Sun.

EAPNLD
EVTE

ODEEYIGNE

FYAISLLK

YHOOBLSA
NEBTEDRH

DNEUTEARLWE
ALEWKVOALT
UOYWNOXKAEN

Tarantula

A booth
Your two-sided arena
One metre by one metre
Battle the books, the berks and the rawest of data
You are now a professional coffee annihilator

Your legs crunched like numbers
Your back hunched like a question mark
Tendons crooked with cramp
But you're fine
The company said so
Just thirty years to go
You'll suffer like a pro

The vending machine
Sugar and sanity
Sucking away a few moments of the day
Overtime against credit card vanity
Back to your booth
A life lived in quiet desperation
Tarantula

Etrosion 21

Muddled, muddied and beguiled,
Ill with inconsistencies,
Rushed through normalized commitment,
Harrowing deadlines and unholy harp.

Hung off-kilter with blithe border,
An Etrosion,
Outdone, numbed and numbered.

Willowed with an unnerving sharpness,
Papercutting between the toes,
Trembling under imaginable weight,
A Portrait of betrayal,
Hand crafted with arthritic crank,
Posing fragile and failed.

Soulless

We reverse engineer and dilute life's soul
Forget the extravagant and mock up monstrous
Collective pride is no longer a goal

Splash scruffy in un-ironed shoal
Decency and manners no longer on the syllabus
We reverse engineer and dilute life's soul

Once all workers not piners for the doll
Hold open a door without anyone to prompt us
Collective pride is no longer a goal

Community spirit stood when life took its toll
To not offer your seat would seem preposterous
We reverse engineer and dilute life's soul

Sensible change is no longer a cross on the poll
Public services rarely prompt or conscientious
Collective pride is no longer a goal

Cluttered contemporary skyline drab and droll
A smile and a nod no longer in the subconscious
We reverse engineer and dilute life's soul
Collective pride is no longer a goal

Uncomfortable

Back to work after scissored barnet
With hairy neck collared burn

Winter duvet, a month too early
Clammy bedsheets toss and turn

Last minute late cinema booking
Premier show front row mecha-neck crank

Early twentics first time mortgage application
Thirty-five-year fear waiting room dock bank

Spring day and sticky arms
Leather jacket, short sleeve t-shirt underneath

Mid-calf paddle, semi-towelled
Beach sand spiked trainer feet

Smog living room air, down-putting talk
Sinister discreet scowls, unpleasant comments

I eggshell walk

Shrapnel

Oversized whiskey bottle
Chump change
Cobwebbed in the corner
Railing to reach work
An electric train pain
Throne of prat on the roof
Ill-judged
Wasted opportunity climate aloof

Just a matter of time
Before the track n' trace tricksters
Pin stripe power tie hipsters
Claim to choke on cow field fart
Scythe our great produce providers
Just like when they ripped out Sri Lanka's heart

Eerie erratic economy pledge
The CAT scan room door held open
Jammed with fictional untraceable wedge
Those loose coins will collide
Tearing through Fleet Street meat
Bankers in their bunkers
Parliament pedantic
Our green and pleasant land
Freefalling, food-banked, afraid and frantic

Jolly Green Giants

Let's go good!
Let's go green!
Daily we walk above treasures unseen
The parties adamant, renewable by 2033
But it's no longer turbulent turbine sea
Let's push it and probe
Use a white robe
Nudge the people
The public simple and feeble
Radio antenna church steeples
SAVE GOD'S GLORIOUS EARTH!
Out to the masses
Infiltrate all school, college and Uni' classes
Stealth it in
Copper and tin
Our new Bronze Age
Flatten a million Chilean homes
Overlords observe from peacock coal thrones
Burrow deep and burrow vile
Prance and parade in ozone-provoc' style
Let's do good!
Let's dig further!
We'll all die on this large green Bunsen burner!

Kensington Avenue

Many can only brag
About a bag of bric-a-brac
Convenience stores that once thrived
Now coatless and emotionless
The Philly rain
Drench opioid brains

Oblivious blues just flutter by
This hornet hive
Stop signs and the untitled
Plastic quarry park steps
Fire hydrant showers
Needle meds

A city that never sleeps
As it zombies and tweaks
Someone's son
Someone's daughter
Kicked to the curb by the minted
Lambs to the slaughter
Denied help when they needed it most
Punching away at paper bag ghosts

On prosperous cleaner streets
The Avenue is a phrase never to be uttered
Leather belts between blackening enamel
Camp chairs against spray paint shutter

Dolly

There may be more, feneckling amongst us.
Goose necking, hydroplaning on time; the house's funds.
In similar vein.
I wonder, are they our equal, are they better?
Fine-tuned and ambidextrous, whilst brushing borrowed
teeth, rolling onto their right side with lamp Shatterhand.
Do they sleep at all?
Wooing with fraudulent form and parasite smile;
Greeting extended family in the hallway mirror, whilst
style stealing familiar scarf and hat.
Do they move with lab finesse, genetic jitterbugging to
my tune at a party?
Were we to meet, would they acknowledge with a
symmetrical nod? Run perhaps?
Would they thank me?
Am I sufficient?

As Is

I participate
I'm not fearless, but fear little
I'm an unwilling participant of a day long and laced with
glass slither disappointments.
The sternum flick of chance or change lasts but a
moment.
Flatlining along
the highs but a ripple, the lows cavernous troughs.

I participate
Ignoring the overwhelming weight.
The twist of the screw's elephantine memory.
Reckless abuse of dopamine use relieves the burdens of
the toxic mind.

I affiliate
with similar souls, crowbarring the door to a city of
sense, where civility still strolls.

I participate
Like a coalmine canary
with an unheard heads up whilst others breath buried.
Upwards swiping with agreeable thumb instead of
hitchhiking out of Dodge.

I participate
They ponder
But, As Is, does not pander.

Bungee

Took a blockbuster honeycombed diagonal
Whilst the hangers-on got caught in the grenadine
All sincerely serial killer sorry
Chips on shoulders saltier than ever
With rock band fade away guy fame
Indulging by the bag
Digging for the riff

Rainy days of palates
Bourbon by the fifth
Sipped months premature
A moonshine America cup-melter
Liquid pool pleasure floor
Although the yellow sign invited the slip
No insurance my sausage?
Your savings for your new hip

The wound infected with soda park dreams
Smog power station down by the sea
Rip cord cordial sobriety
A thousand and one ways to grunt
Check the squires haven't snipped that rope
Before you take that crucifix jump

Nihilism by Mouth

Infinite dorms, unknown sparsity
No-clipped here with irritable glitch
Dark tepid tiles, cluster bomb carpet
Vacant apartment, tube light switch

Tinkle Ode to Joyless
Acid aesthetics and familiarity
Timeless replication melancholia
Liminal space hauntology

No future stairwells
Meaningless cookie cutter walls
Abandoned amusement parks
Clinical school locker halls

Fortuneless garage forecourts
Covid strolls at night
The senile, the sleazy and the sleuth
Breezeblock pastures and flickering light

'Orrid office spaces to rent
Audios ambling, footsteps and fear
Lack of reason or barter in these backrooms
No rules, laws or logic to adhere

Doubting purpose and it's plightful panache
Applied traits inked and branded on
We're good, we're bad, we begin, we end
Life drip-fed and meaningless until the bitter end

Massacre

The hedges desperately need massacring,
But I'll do it later in the year,
Birds' nests I do fear.
But here comes a highway's tractor,
Complete with cutting gear,
I know, shear madness I hear!

They desperately need massacring.

Synchronicity

Pause.

Take a solitary moment
Disconnect and reconnect
There's a less turbulent terminal

It's the petulance of the wasp
The lone robin who braves your companionship
That cloud that haunts with delightful disfigurement
The nonplus of a rain droplet
A song on the radio reminiscent of burdens surpassed
A beach stone pick that shimmers too much for the skim
The incredulity of a reach out from an unsent letter
The crawl of an ant across handwritten page

Pause.

Take a moment

Dot to dot, all signs the misguided forgot

The 4:15 Kick

It's the 4:15 kick
A reflection pixelates back
With wounded intent
As, in my pudding proof
Tainted compass signposts ignored
Pale at my gulag-self

It's the 4:15 kick
Too late to sleep
Too early to rise
Slag-silt silk guilt
Dilate crust in the corner of my eyes

Accepted the discarded seeds
Chicken-feed scattered
Fermented rye throat
Improvising and make-doing
Ends meet with lacklustre cope
Zero-hour cash in hand hustle
A needle of light named Hope

Bic to the neck is not vanity
But to stifle the burrow ingrowth
But the cold razor has its way
Leaving a pristine path
Wherever it foam slides
Wiping the past, bar slight stubble rash
And an Adam's nick profanity

A mechanism against wildfire
A design of control and erase
I keep my cabinet
Of pills and pointys closed
Particularly on raincloud days

It's the 4:15 kick
My abode is current
Open plan, shuttered curtains
The letterbox creak-snaps
With overactive spittle
An envelope mound of menace
Sharp paper lick-sealed
With rent truant tenant tongue
Stagnant soaked teacups
Nightol, No-fucks and Netflix

It's the 4:15 kick
Winter, mid-month sometime
I wish they could just see me
If I ever make my prime

There Shall Be No Place

There shall be no place
For the bile and the abusers
The bathers as shallow as the river
The botherers and the blinkered
Baiters and blatant haters
Acid instigators
Eel ankle aggressors
Yanking at our ascent
Harming hope
Weighting our float
Surface suppressors
Torniquet tightening tyrants
And when finally we manage to gasp
We gasp
Bubbled, bleeding and bent
Our mouths are appled
And we are silver served
There shall be no place

Bones and Tar

It's within them moments of darkness
Rolling over like a hillside mist
Oh, how I do long, to right everybody's wrong
And methodically tick them off my shit-list

This bubbling, frantic, frenzied whirlpool
A desolate ocean floor of bones and tar
They may never know, of the ugliness down below
As they pleasure boat across my reservoir

I'm just a cog in a machine, a face in the crowd
With an exterior that wouldn't say 'boo' to a goose
That's their first mistake, trying to paddle in my lake
Throw me stale bread and set this hunger loose

Fickle and foolish foes and friends
I socialise through gritted teeth and hidden sneer
One day they'll get a surprise
When I'm mimicked and patronized
And the Devil's razor, scalpels them from ear to ear!

X

Close the blinds, shut out the night,
Cautiously peek through a chink to be sure,
It's just a matter of time, before she commits a crime,
I lock, chain and deadbolt my front door.

With litter strewn and scattered across my lawn,
Grouched through my bin like a sneaky urban fox,
No surprise, to see your Great White shark eyes,
Cold and dead at my letter box.

I truly miss shops, even trolleys and busy crowds,
The festive buzz of sales, snow and stalls,
I rely on friends sometimes, the rest I get online,
Nails blunt from clawing at these walls.

Three jobs, three homes, three years,
A nomadic fleeting and brittle existence,
Never been so scared, of someone who said they cared,
She's my unshakable shadow of sinister persistence.

Today I shuddered, an abysmal letter of hatred,
Coiled with malice under my windscreen wiper,
No longer do I know what to do,
To dissolve her rancid glue,
As she rattles from the undergrowth like a viper.

Gorgeous beaming radiant rays,
Kiss my powder complexion with welcomed heat,
A lung of clear safe sea air,
Salt breeze through neglected hair,
Golden sand serenades carpet weary feet.

So very eager and excited to finally see you today,
Four torrid years and the time has finally come,
As I'm perched up high in a sand dune,
Whistling a jolly tune,
Ready to catch a final glimpse,
Through the sighting on my gun.

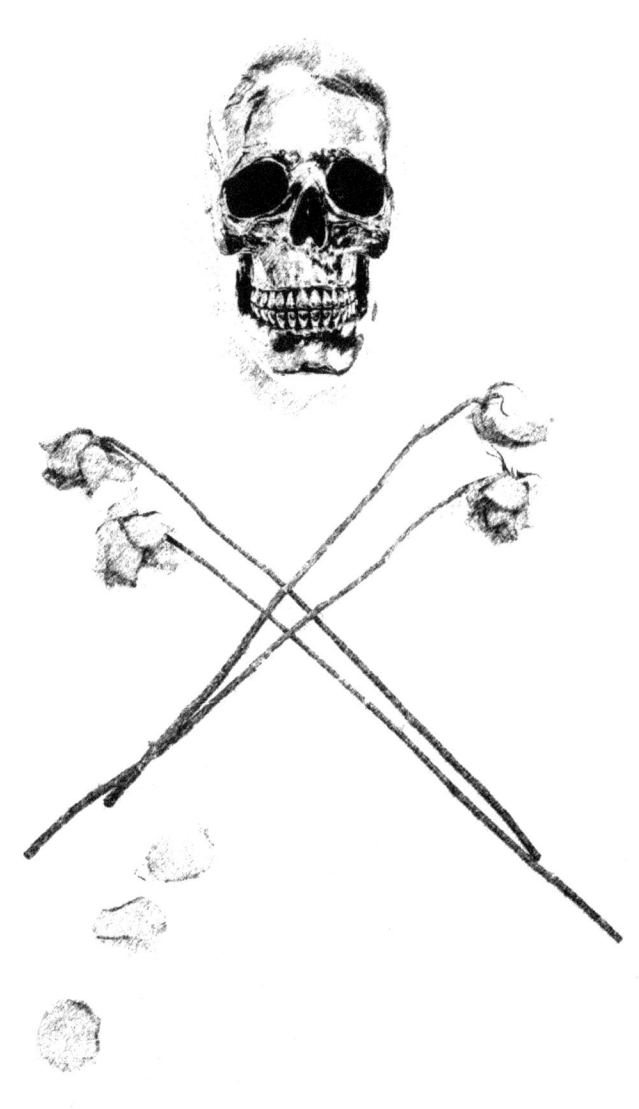

Mr Preegles

He lives alone does Mr Preegles,
A house on Swampchurch Lane,
Watches from porthole attic window,
With litmus peepers of pain.

He's widowed-peaked and widowed,
With nails plectrum sharp,
Muses with dust mites and the crows,
And is always up at first dark.

Sleeps below un-crucifixed headboard,
Closets of capes and fur,
A slithering of awards on B-movie mantlepiece,
Surround a candled urn, of her.

Tired floorboards creak underfoot,
As the boards he once graced,
The greats he once knew, and he knew a few,
Slip his memory and can no longer be placed.

A gaggle of kids with urban legend lunchboxes,
Taunt and titter from the safe side of the fence,
At the glass he arrives punctually with playful menace,
As his daily creep show once again, does commence.

94!

Danger Will Robinson!
Let's just thrown on a projector pipe ban
Dinghy the iconoclastic
Behind a classifuckation dam

Churn them out bland and grand
We forgot the 70's grit, depth and feel
Reduced to line change jingle jerks
Two adults please and one veal

A sequel threequel prequel quadrilogy
Another nacho-dog-buttered-sweet-cola more
Before the walls finally broke
And all the good folk awoke
Welcome to the killing floor of 94!

Cardiac College

Shuffle, slump, sloth and slouch
Every solitary heel dragging day
Belittled, belly-ached, bewildered and blistered
Abysmal walls of Pythagoras grey

Please, let there be a fire in the hole
Please, let there be a non-formulary method to this madness
A tried test subject with patience tested
I'll eventually scarper without a molecule of sadness

Shed the tie and the tie that binds
Cull the cripples that taught me to limp
Totem pole the textbooks and light up a toast
Unclip the wings and let me love, live and think

The defibrillator belted at my Seattle-bound chest
Herman Munstered me onto Doc martin feet
I lank haired and loitered with easel eccentrics
Canoodled and Swaggered with celery chomp teeth

I was oyster oozing from a shackled shell
Brush-prized open, un-lemoned and forever better
In ninety-six I knitted with phonograph needles
And I'll always proudly wear that sweater

Two Footed Challenge

My lotion lathered
With cologne eye sting stigma
Dax wax toucan toupee
Tonight, Matthew…
Label me 'lone wolf sigma'

Top Man wristband
Polo collar unnecessarily up
I've done both press ups and turn ups
Just order me the Julius Caesar salad
First tatt cheap indigo black
Upper arm cost-cutter Triad

Thursday November night in Notts
Ice cutter nipples, no coat
Green frog cocktails and chilli shots
Another potent Hooch for my dry throat
No need to loiter at the left lion
I'm hitting it alone
One pound fifty snakebite with Scream card
Rock City, The Rig and The Zone

I somehow get lassoed into a round
The old rugby posse
Multiple drinks to be pound
They're turbo shandy Sinatras
Bottle's-a-buck-Berlin's
Tape them to my fingers
And do Edward fizzer hands
And Chug!
Last one to the line gets next round
The mug!

Wobble into a late bar
Three for the road
This place is rent-a-throat!
If my sticky soles will let me
I'm getting out of here
Tattoine Cantina central
In a basement of BO, funny smoke and plastic beer.

Fashionista

A fashion parlour prowler
A velten on the verge
On the market for a salvation piece
Avant-garde TK-tickled and jumble submerged
Salt n' pepper sideburns
Solar ceramic watch
He has to watch his ticker on occasion
When a closing down sale drops!

Reaching towards the sun
Darts player silver knuckles and glossy nails
But to no avail
Quartz movement fail
No buying boundaries
No condiment qualms
Bull leathered body
And corduroy arms.

This fashionista gets name-checked in The Nag's
Walk-in wardrobe of fake designer tags
Store card statements up to his nads
An overpriced coffee and a sea of shopping bags.

When in Roam

The   Jan'   sale   tent   dripped

The   seam   split   shell   ripped

The   front   door   went   unzipped

The   cold   flask   coffee   unsipped

Sheer   crap   storm   flap

Mole   lump   bad   back

Partner   tries   to   bite   her   lip

Marks   of   a   great   camping   trip

Be   safe   be   seen   fluro   orange

Mid   peak   Welsh   speak   up   Blorenge

No   gas   mud   paths   let's   forage

Weird   cherry   obscure   berry   in   porridge

Thumbed screen ramblers app'
Glovebox glitch forgotten map
We've ended up bloody miles from home
All been Darted, no freedom to roam!!

Bricks and Mortar

It may seem sparce, daunting, damp and bland,
Staring over half an acre of fresh virgin land,
Pondering dreamhouse potential,
As they deliver gravel, slabs and sand,
From here on out it's up to you,
Slum in a shed or choose Chateaux Grand?

Research builders, take your time, select well,
There are many a bad tradesman out there,
Who'll make your life a living hell,
For every great castle built, another great castle fell,
But sometimes the cracks are minor and repairable,
Think before you sell.

Topcoat that fence, seed and water luscious lawn,
Paint bold, bright and beautiful,
Decorate to adorn,
Plan and prepare, bricks and mortar,
Skips, brain and brawn,
You've been in this mortgage of life,
Since the very day that you were born.

I know not all cement is mixed the same,
But I'm afraid that you're the architect,
So there's nobody else to blame,
"But my land wasn't flat!"
Come on, that's just lame!
You're responsible for keeping yourself out of the rain.

Some day's the breeze blocks stagger and cause a tilt,
Pressures will force wooden beams to wilt,
But stand tall, firm and strong,
Hosepipe away any gritty grime and silt,
So grow, extend, convert,
Live in the house you have proudly built!

Pine

The jumble billboard, jig-sawed and rain fractured in the rear-view, sits like an old album cover memory. The surviving slits of light devoured by cat's eyes. Heavy lids tick along with the wipers.
Tongue coffee'd, feet leaded and brain sludge'd. The off-ramp sirens with a chorus of perhaps. I continue, uncharted, glue-pawed and persistent.

The station crackles with hybrid, as my cell intrudes for the umpteenth, illuminating denim worn upholstery. My surroundings are glanced as the layered asphalt behind distances and thins with every tyre spindle.
White lamps eyeball judgingly on passing. Misfits switch, swish and swoosh under an amber flicker fever.

Motel neon forces through scattered sporadic shrubs, tormenting a signpost to shadow a hangman-like shadow on lit granite overpass.

Our flow; briefly encumbered by lane lion, hungry to red-blue elk and filterers with witching hour shred.
Stars appear to work in tandem as gas stations callously consort, pranking my progress.

Idling by a log tariff eighteen-wheeler, I'm gifted a nose of diesel that duels my swinging perfumed pine.
I push as I pine for redwoods. Reposeful yet towering; a cullis to smalltown quaintness, an antidote to regrettable concrete pasts.

Pudding pocket

It's a Mixer-Maxer-Juicer-Grinder-Coffee Fellator
Ideal for all hard work haters
De-kitsch that kitchen
Impressss
All-in-one, a million others can't be wrong?!
Top of the range, end of the line
Until the very end of time
Dial quick before your chance is gone!
Here's our hypnotic host with the most, who sirens with dazzling redrum dentures. Get ready to be seduced by an over-friendly demeaning demeanour
They thoroughly recommend
They have one of their own
It's the showpiece of their home
Don't suffer alone
Purchasssse
Welcome to the Shopping Zone!
But **WAIT!!**
That's not all.
Pay in thirteen instalments and for everyone's enthrallment: a complimentary carriage clock!
Clearly not dispensable overstock.
Number below…just caaalllll

You feel that burn
The credit card rotisserie turn
Like an over-microwaved syrup pudding
Melting pocket thread, ready to bake your bread
But it's all completely fine
Cyan Sea Glitter Ghost Trillionaires Club Polo luggage and jeans are next inline!

Hello…yes, my credit card number is…

Twickenham

I walk, a warrior amongst my tribe,
Red rose chested and ready,
Thoroughly hydrated,
Throff still on lips, moustache and stubble,
Here, there is no such thing as crowd trouble.

The hot breath from my chips,
Swirls into the cool autumn air,
A salt and vinegar smoke single,
Oh how my eyes do sting,
But that is instantly forgotten,
When the fans begin to sing.

There she stands, our fortress, our Colosseum,
With my ticket clutched, like a stunned fly,
I begin my ascent of a thousand steps,
A spider spectator climbing a Webb Ellis,
But there's a buzz in the air, a feeling like no other,
Eighty-two thousand friends, sisters and brothers.

A sea of stark white shirts,
I'm approached by a ghostbuster,
Business makes him feel good,
An ammo stack of plastic pints on proton pack,
He better watch his footing,
Especially with five litres of ale on his back.

The pitch, oh the pitch,
Hair scissor trimmed and horizon flat,
Golf putting citrus green,
To bruise with thirty boots,
Sacrilege, crude and obscene.

Out the Gladiators roll to chorus,
Then..
The Anthems,
A synchronized standing heartfelt din,
I have to bring beer to lips and gulp, to mask my gulp,
As I contemplate a series win.

The whistle, a thud of boot,
As the ovel launches high,
Tickling the belly of the clouds of Heaven,
Then plummeting to the clatter of shields,
As one army lay claim,
And the sun is so very persistent,
Rays of blessing down onto God's game,

Twickenham.

Spider On a Recce

Let's get set and wobble the web
Peep and check the coast is clear
Looks like the whole family are in
Just as I bloody well feared!

But a spider like me must Parker up
Give this gauntlet a jolly good go
Only a lounge and hall before the kitchen
To reach a juicy fly in the rear window

I scuttle start lightning quick
Out over the arm of a chair
But accidentally terrify sister in the process
Who launches coffee and laptop in the air

A reactive leap to a safety curtain
A death defying abseil to the ground
Out comes monster movie mutt
Who growls, snarls and tsunami slobbers around

I hear dad bellow 'It won't hurt you!'
In an idle attempt to defuse
But it's only because he can't hear the telly
And missing the cricket scores on the news

Beelining across the hallway
Dancing brother's size twelve stomp feet
He ignores calls of 'Get that spider!'
He's off out, beer to drink and mates to meet

Then a hiss from an evil evasive presence
A cellar spider vows 'You shall not pass'
Well, more fool him, as I shoot him a little grin
And mid-dinner mother traps him with a glass

Finally blanching eyes, on a delicious well-earned treat
Just moments from being bluebottle fed
As for the family, I'll be getting my own back later
By walking over their faces, whilst all asleep in bed.

Hokey Dina!

She jet set with hurricane heal hilt
Dragged them stompers along with spardo-sesame
Jenga Jowell jackets of crushed felt
Championed a double spread chip shop paper obituary

In her eventual passing, we remember her passin'
Oozing with clotted clesso authority
With the wolves a -whistlin' and the Lunas a-howlin'
The masses necessed with bruised cervix certainty

She was gazel gerdy, flamenco fire fine
A loose lasso-lipped lickety-split host
In her properdoppel prime, always eloquently dined
Now she radoodles in your room, the classy wet ghost

Pro Rata Tomatoes

By another twist of fate,
You're propositioned real late,
If you question or refuse they'll become irate,
Even guilt you ghoulies,
'Put more food on the family plate'
The shithouse will even pretend to be your mate,

The overtime overture.

My coat was on and zipped,
And just about to clock out,
From the fiery head office depths,
Came that blood curdling shout,
"Middle-management infiltrate all exits!"
"Sorry son there's no way out!"
Easily forgotten time in lieu available no doubt,

The pro rata tomatoes

Dawkin Kettleton's Spuds

Dawkin Kettleton's spuds were bad
He tried to mash'em
Butter'em
Gave'em a scrub
Still didn't come up any good

Dawkin Kettleton's spuds were bad
He tried to de-soil'em
Baking foil'em
Gave'em a peel
He really should've given'em a good feel

Dawkin Kettleton's spuds were bad
He tried to hash brown'em
Air-fry'em
Whisk'em with cream
Even worse you should've seen Dawkin Kettleton's aubergine!

BOLT

If they piss down your back and tell you it's raining,
Drop their arse in the room they just came in,
Dig up the garden you've spent years maintaining,
Better bolt or bolt the door!

Hiding in your attic, hole in the ceiling,
Better
Numb your nuts with nitrogenous feeling,
Bolt
Come along for the ride but start freewheeling,
Or
If sickly suspicious affection glops congealing,
Bolt
Their crucible crowd become bolshy and unappealing,
The
Chops off ya' bonce instead of knighting when kneeling,
Door!
So get armour-suited and sabot-booted,
Wrench out Excalibur and go Medievalin'!

Photostagenic

An obsessive click collector,
In an arrowroot sweater,
No faddy digital SLR,
View camera and hood work better.

A lavender luddite tie,
A tittering tongue that never lies,
An annual subscription to side-parting weekly,
A larder of Bentos steak n' kidney pies.

Farah's break correctly at the top of his shoe,
A cellar dweller, trains, paint and model glue,
Coat placed over puddles on his few twilight dates,
Didn't plaster a Paris until nearly thirty-two.

Toothbrush steriliser, multi hand gel positioner,
Dapper barnet 'oh fiddlesticks' practitioner,
Vitamins, prayers and well hoovered stairs,
When terrestrial left, he became a wireless listener.

Only supports local with a hatred of crowds,
Raps on the wall when neighbours are loud,
Trims garden and moustache with hairdresser scissors,
Disinfects, dusts daily, homely house proud.

Novels shelved alphabetically, vintage and eccentric,
Pushbike in the hallway, 70's Raleigh authentic.

Ready for the Ride

I've scoured the bathtub
With detol-intervention
Scum lines rithered
Kicked the egg into touch
Beam slipped into quicksand
Dragged my clay beast self out
Clawed at collapsible slate
Held aloft prayer, tongue and bowl
Until the end of a drought

Nudged into nettles and napalmed
Dockless, near lifeless, but never made a fuss
Knocked square pegs into round holes
Been both penniless and flush

Franticked around the block
On a breathless bus
Picked up my gnashers
Picked up my bloody gnashers
Signalled the driver to **stop!**
With two fingers up

Life has teeth
Nibbling until the wreath
Been there, bit that!
Eventually when the pistons pound out
Oil tepid, mileage maxed
I'll camber back on the workshop floor
The light will be non-hesitant green
With sunroof smile and journeys to my dial
I'm ready for the ride

Oval

I feared it was in the post
The signature headaches
Years of barrelling towards the posts
Missing words and line breaks

Punt it into space
Forgetfulness was never my thing
As I stare into space
Stud headed sin bin

Childhood parties I can't remember

Pre-season contact training

Kick off September

Loud Silence

Sometimes silence is loud
Everyone's out
The dog sleeps
He hiccups and snores occasionally
An old lamp irritates
Like a fly
With monotonous hum
The heating's been off
Even the washing machines done
The silence has its own identity
Its own din today

As I procrastinate
And my mind lurks
Temples buzz with nothingness
Melancholia raises a snide smirk
I never fret
It comes and goes in soundwaves
Sooner or later, I'll be occupied
Distracted
Life loud
And this poem can be retracted

A Breezy Poem

You can hear the truth in the wind,
As it flays the corn,
Breezes violet field,
Valley and carcass,
Claxons the moor,
Pummels the hiker and torments the angler,
Loads the float with false hope.

You can hear the voice of the wind,
Groans the chimney stack,
Teeth chatters the letterbox
Kettle whistles the vent
Paper tear scare your tent.

You can feel the pride in the wind,
As it grapples against your front door,
Oppresses a fairway drive,
Wiggles fence post footing,
Visits your lawn bearing litter strewn gifts.

You should fear the wind's wrath,
Angering oceans,
Sea weed stone wall aftermath,
A vengeful Wurlitzer lifting barns
Bargaining lives like Texas Holdem chips.

Medusa

Minimal dark oak coffee truffle
Table brittle bare
Polished to a lake
Reflections of the highly decorated
Executives of extortion
Prefects perspire with their reports
Papers marked with claret quill

Silence

A shuffle. A symphony
A throat clear. A throttle
A misjudged answer an atrocity
Over two-tiered balcony
Cloak and dagger falconry

The host a shadowy Medusa
A single vacant chair
A poisonous position
A proposition with an octopus band
The absent, the agent

Ballot in with knife toe
Ballot in with Steel smile
Ballot in with razored rim

An interpreter eye-lashed and orderly
An auditor with tentacle reach
Hot coals under MI6 feet

Intruder

Leaping through a tree, branch to branch
Vaulting over the garden gate
Navy-rolling into the shadows
Where he lay patiently in wait

The security cam swung into a blind spot
The perfect moment to try his luck
Targeting a second-floor window
Clambering brick with a grappling hook

He stealthily Grasshopper'd along the hall
To the bedroom straight ahead
Then snuck chocolates onto a dressing table
That stood at the foot of the bed

He was then startled by headlights and engine
As the returning owner gravelled onto the drive
So, taking a chance, getting wet through to his pants
Into the backyard swimming pool, he swan-dived

As he surfaced, many cops had arrived
Surrounded, no chance of getting away
With surrendering hands he pleaded with an officer
"But, its only because the lady loves Milk Tray!"

"You can tell that one to the Judge" He sneered
"You're lucky you weren't pumped full of lead"
"But I want to be the next James Bond!" He cried
"Too late; they already gave that to Big Fry instead"

Morse Code

A lovely little booth adjacent to the bar
A centrepiece and cocktail menu to impress
Plenty **O**f **F**olk around, a lively teatime crowd
In case I need to signal for help, or yell **S.O.S**

You glitter-saunter in, fashionably late
At the very least you resemble your profile
Within twenty years of advertised age
Unlike "I've just not updated my pics for a while"

I breezy chat, but you're stern from the off
A few flags we may not get along
You balk at my one-liners, you talk like an old-timer
Screw your face like tasting batteries with your tongue

To a sneer and sigh of **AA** disapproval
I've the tenacity to order drink number two
She's entitled, crypt boring and bar staff rude
At least Sky Sports is over her shoulder just in view

She lectures off strict requirements and her five-year plan
A move, money, marriage and thrice up the duff
I'll nip to the bathroom and escape out of a window
At least for once I wasn't labelled just 'A bit of rough'

The Warmth of Galahad

A throat drieth,
Neck tie of burden,
Accomplished thy shit of shift,
Flagon thirst of certain.

An Inn of peasant ensemble,
Fiddle jukebox beast of monstrous sound,
A welcome hand-pull, from ale maiden of bust,
I perch nobly on table of round.

Their arrival, fashionably of late,
Via Uber of irons and dragon of rail,
Bearing kitty courtesy of Uncle Arthur,
A raised toast, to himself…we Hail!!

Sir Percival pigs on scratchings of hog,
As a laughing Lancelot jests and bards,
Bedivere banters with Boris The Younger,
And Merl' entertains with magic trick of cards.

Loungeroom Love

Let's not play one another off
Like pen pal fools
We're just two paragliders in the storm
I've got the slip-ons and you've got the tools

A soirée with a firepit
And a fire in my heart
We're just two cubes in a good malt
Crackling Bacharach and Bauhaus art

Apologies on my stylophone approach
I can be a little coy
The scent of pledge and pussycats
I promise I'm not like other girls and boys

Necking under the mistletoe
In my cashmere rollneck
When two wrapping paper scissor-sliders collide
Amongst eggnog, sherry and Christmas decs'

My soul, caramel to the quick
Just give me the wink
And I'll twist the lid off this dancefloor jam jar

…Help me baby, I think I'm corked!

Let the talkers talk
I don't give a crisp pastry fork
Yesterday, today, today, yesterday are different days
With asteroids in your eyes let's Galaxy walk

Let me whisper with carmth
Feel my polyester patter garter goo
We're just two sides of the gold chocolate coin
Listen to your tingles, they tickle the truth

Let's blow kisses with trumpet cheeks
Like cream filled horns on the bandstand
We're just two unravelling iced cinnamon buns
Let's crêpe with well-floured hands

…Come on in baby, The patisseries open!

Red Curtain Call

Mermaid treasure eyes and sand. A town of splinters and plastic. The treble of mill saws and the tremble of a paw that grinds the volume, to a shattering pitch, a shriek of tortured souls.
Taken souls,
Some borrowed,
Some buried.
Sugar rush doughnuts, shrouded by coffee, sweet tooth the room from engine oil ears. It's much more than marijuana melodrama promiscuous prom…
She welcomes the debauchery night after night after night. Cleansing away her remaining slats of innocence, that still may keep her window latch open.

And her heels…! kcilC

Saturn forest absorbs through dark pores,
Amongst glasto hail-shade sycamores,
Where the light is porcupined by peril,
The savage, the imposter and the morally feral,
Lick the garmonbozia spoon,
Under Bob's revolting moon,
That finger jams the throat and struttle,
With spoilt jazzed hands.
The Venus' hold no arms to be bent backwards,
Unable to mason-shake on brown and white,
All at the lodge's red curtained delight,

And her fingers…! KcilC

Her

Around the decaying ruins I did creep,

Pulling up tattered collar of fur,

The scent of lavender, murder and mirth,

The scent of danger and sweetness…

Her.

Lemon Drizzle Cake

I toy with lemon drizzle cake
Like a Victorian villain
My moustache I do twizzle
My sugar, oh the sugar!
My marrow craves and aches
At your citrus bake

I fork open my lemon drizzle cake
Like a hungered theatrical thesp
My carnal cravat conquest
What perilous pleasures you bring
My fruit, oh the fruit!
Zealous zest!
My wrong, you right everything.

Avec une créme glacée lemon drizzle cake
Like a crude culinary cardinal
My jester teared tart
My vivacious vice, oh vital victual vice!
My sodden acidulous ambrosia
My waistline you do take!

Commune

A desire for ant-static satin cloth stability.
Bone-snapping the mundane. A guide who giveth but divides equally.
Safety netting the tumble.
As humble pie is devoured with satanic munch, we serpent spit out pips of the day to day with mulch, shedding our lizard scales.
Retrieving tired limbs from the quicksand's despair.
Meditate.
Chew off the bear trapped ankle.
Illuminate.
The skies of virtuous potential.
Let not feareth your innerself.
Release the shackles of family, friends and hard-earned wealth. Just giveth, be mindful.
Your guide is completely un-woeful to...
All that bare all,
Under the light,
Behind commune walls
Timber white,
Barbed wired,
Twelve feet in height,
Ownership, greed, money and power,
Is no longer a thing,
No longer a burden,
But maybe it still is to HIM!
Lives altered, deceived and devoted,
As this giver does so sneakily preach,
But for goodness sake,
Don't make the mistake,
Drinking refreshments laced with bleach!

Cooper

The timepiece, the screech and the scatter
The balaclavas, the blueprint and the bank
The lookout, the looters and the leader
The unnoticed, the off-duty Officer and the oath
The badge, the bullets and the bloodshed
The screams, the sirens and the surround
Faces of hockey mask grimace
As they surrender face down on the ground

But not here…
Yes, there was fear, but…
November 21st, 1971
A non-portly man
From Portland
Purchased a 'One way ticket if you please'
With a best laid plan
Smart, brylcreamed, polite and at ease
Single cube scotch
Narrow tie and automatic watch
Typewritten folded note
That converted a lipstick smile to a frown
All passengers released after brief touchdown
Back up to a smooth cruise, at low altitude
A bomb bluff, four parachutes and Reno bound
Over southwest Washington he stepped out for some air
Skydiving D.B Cooper is still yet to be found

Hellova Novella

The further you solve
The more it hurts
Unearthly engineering
Prove your commitment
Like the novella in your hand
It prickles and purrs
Weaves with scalpel configuration
Paragraph chunks

Areola evil gel
Unfathomable sights
Dry penetration sound
Read, read
Come, read aloud
Semen release breadcrumb trails
Each chapter enslaves and impales
Eager beaver pleasure and pain
Strike with barbed hook
Winch out your appetites
And leave the rats your remains

You opted for the story
Treasures unseen
Unlike bland library shelf lobotomy
Pleasures sadistic, pulsing and mean
Your skinless skeletal crawl
Absorbs the putrid
Evolving with every pulp turn
Forbidden fruit downfall

It chose you
Indulge
There's no going back
As they whisper the sinner and bite from the black
Gliding forward and towering over
Whilst you cross-legged prism pose
The pegged, the woeful, the weak and the willer
You've been own tarot card dealer

Sandpapered that itch
Peeling back the puzzle
Giddy and gushing
Cretin pleasure bitch
Wounds that may never heal
Temptations of the flesh intrigue
Devoured in one sitting, one serving, one meal

Twisting at your incisors with ruthless precision
And unhygienic voluptuous flare
They'll untangle, rewire, re-route your filth
As your sickly serenade
Taunts their leather infused parade
With red hand clammed around papercut spine
Bells tinkle, bulbs flicker
Walls shift, cogs turn
Your hell bound heart pounds quicker
Trembling hesitantly over the final line…
It's their barbed wire hammock now
Face to face with their glass shard embrace

As you realise now… is your time!

Love is a Rabid Dog

Love is a rabid dog that must be fed
It likes to fuck, and it likes to be bred
Punctures the muscle with fangs
Latches with staffie-strength jowl
When in need it whimpers and howls

It digs deep with bone marrow treat
Muddies the sofa and interferes with sleep
Contents Infront of an open fire
On a dreary drizzled night
Protects its family and territory
With ferocious mongrel fight

Doesn't ever judge or mock
When their master's right or wrong
And you'll always miss the mutt
When it's finally forever gone

Witness Me!!

I was a war pup rev-head
Ate porridge from a V8 plate
Daydreaming of chrome and carburettors
Guzzolene, guts and war-rig freight

I'd just hit NutraSweet sixteen
Cue-ball bald and powder white
Slumped in my blood bag bunk
Contemplating this Kamikaze life

I'm Valhalla and my saviour
Right through to carbon core
Although there's a slight spanner in the works
There's something I now cherish more

A bad-land survival seductress
An Imperator of dust mirage
A pedal to the metal Princess
An outback angel leading supply run charge

I imagine an alternate rising sun
If I were to ever have my way
Proposing with sprocket, from rusty pocket
Making plans for our wasteland wedding day

Recite our vows on Citadel plinth
Her mechanical hand in mine
I'd stare into her engine oil striped eyes
Two petrol-head partners in crime

The hordes of the wretched would whistle and chant
Whilst Coma-Doof played thrash guitar
People Eater, Bullet Farmer and the Gas Town guys
Would all journey from afar

My best man Nux, in chainmail tux,
Ushers of Erectus, Scrotus and Colossus
If on the day, Immortan won't give Furiosa away
I'll polecat an email to Lord Humungus

Farm

He crunches buttered triangles
To dawn's chorus raises a mug
Silicone yellow sun
Pitchfork and grass mound
Tree silhouette and hound
Rose wire worn wears
Moulded muscles and joints that crack
Crow's feet and lambing lines
Shovel hips and milk bucket spine

He fights progress and age
Grasps with mitts of mud
A clinical greenbelt cull
Outpriced but not outdone
Trespass signs and shotgun
Shrub prickly, penniless but proud
Unholy harvest and lockdown lunacy
Scarecrow scowl and loose powerlines
Shovelling shit amongst development crimes

As he spits at their enticer
They accuse him of fork tongue
Promises, pleads and purple cloth
To this he clings and will not move on
Splashing him with well water
Digging in further with every verse
Farming this body further with its seeds
Storm watering before the final drought
One last late harvest of menace
Before they cast it out!

Climbing Frame Fall

A shrewd summer
The gut of July eighty-four
A hysterically packed playground
Was my climbing frame fall

Fearless and carefree at height
Just seconds before my slip
It was the lateral compact thud
That made my mother sick

Sharp tinnitus ears
Feeling and touch almost gone
But the most severe injury
Were the fellow parents that looked on

Blurry stars and bright orbs appeared
In skies without a cloud
Eventually winning the battle of winded lungs
To gasp and scream aloud

In typical child battalion style
I was up, dust-down and ice-creamed
I've always remembered that trip to this day
Many as apathetic as life always seems

Frankie the Fixer

When the surgeon faced the famileoso,
the nervously sincere expression revealed his hand.
Before a single word of condolence or apology was
uttered or said, at precisely twelve minutes past the
witching hour, Frankie the Fixer was officially
pronounced dead.

Once upon a time, his red-lit cobbled corner creator
Decided to be a Catholic Church donator
Rather than visit a back-alley butcher exterminator
He was barely more than a dot
The Nuns adored that tot
Even with scuffed knees and sleeve of snot

At sheaf sixteen he fled the flock
By day he learnt to swindle, hustle and box
By night to drink, debauch and pick locks
Never primed to be a delegate for City Hall
But fists like hams and stood over six feet tall
It wasn't long before he found a family after all

Protection rackets, bars, restaurants and shops
Funding gambling habits of out of shape cops
Petrol bomb rivalry between the pigs, micks and wops
A mobster once held a loaded pistol to his ear
Reciting the hoodlums home address without fear
The thug soon tailed it back to his family in tears

But the beast eventually got the better of him
Too many green cookies from the biscuit tin
Now bloated and slow, once a boxer sharp and slim
Bespoke suits tailored, tastes terrine and fine
Pearl Tablecloth, orange bowl and red wine
When that door burst open, he knew it was his time…

Purgatory, tiepin and gauze
A waiting room for the scared and the sinful
Steeped in revolt, regret and remorse
Angers anchored within
Electric lemonade and hand grenades
The orphaned and widowed dance on his grave
Cement-feeted, liquor treaty
Holding cells, bribes and correlates
Mugshot, slingshot sacred bars
To poem, rhyme and pirouette
Beagle bitches and Regal riches
Many cries with gutless guttural regret
Luciferian slideshow on matchstick eye
Christ's criteria must be met
Rid the circus, crimes and cigarettes
Crushed velvet knees thread-bare
Guilt and despair and nerves shredded
The filth and the gore and the knives imbedded

Here I kneel Frankie the Fixer
With currency of a cleansed soul, I do plead to pay!
A warm door opened alike when basketed on church step
As Cato and The Angels guided him on a newfound way

Safety Pin Heart

Oh editing
I must address
It's grotesque process
They say more is less
More or less
Do as you very well please…
Stick architect rigid with the structure
Or abuse beats, breaks and font
If you want?
But please never cease…
To ink bleed, from a safety pin heart
Cause' sometimes a little anarchy
Makes tremendous art

About

K.M. Littleworth is an English born writer living on the rugged Celtic coastline of the Isle of Man.

With a varied background within Art, Literature, Design and Engineering, he's the author of Doppelgänger: Poems & Prose.

A creator, craftsman, world builder, music head, rambler, climber, dog lover and a bit of a beach bum; he's rarely to be found without a pen, pencil, paintbrush, paddle or plectrum in grasp.

For more information on further projects, upcoming appearances, events, slams and signings; visit the official author site: www.kmlittleworth.com

2023 Safety Pin Heart

www.ingramcontent.com/pod-product-compliance
Lightning Source LLC
Chambersburg PA
CBHW051601010526
44118CB00023B/2783